Mark Wood

Michael Terence
Publishing

First published in paperback by
Michael Terence Publishing in 2021
www.mtp.agency

Copyright © 2021 Mark Wood

Mark Wood has asserted the right to be identified as the
author of this work in accordance with the
Copyright, Designs and Patents Act 1988

ISBN 9781800941212

No part of this publication may be reproduced, stored in
a retrieval system, or transmitted, in any form or by
any means, electronic, mechanical, photocopying,
recording or otherwise, without the prior
permission of the publishers

Cover images
Copyright © Pavle MatiÄ‡
www.123rf.com

*I would like to thank all the
CEOs, Business Partners and Private Equity Groups
that I have worked with over the years
which has enabled me to share this career journey.*

Contents

Introduction 1

1: Back in the Beginning 3

2: Life Begins… 13

3: Entering National But Followed By Mistakes 31

4: It All Changed From Here… 41

Mark Wood

Introduction

June 2020: A sunny summers day after the UK has had a major lockdown due to the global pandemic, Covid-19, and consistent bad news daily. For the past few months, my motivation and determination has been nothing but positivity and bright future thoughts. For so many days during the past months I have not stopped thinking about how lucky I am, but then realised it has been down to my determination over many years of hard work and aspirations of getting results. I kept coming back to… I did it, but it took time. There began my thoughts of thinking, anyone can do it, no matter what the challenges in life, U really can do it. There was the start of me looking back over 30-35 years of what and how I did it. I should put it all on paper to inspire others that are in school after such challenge's students have faced and will continue to face in the next year or two.

I am pleased to welcome you to my world of…

U Can Do It!

1:
Back in the Beginning

Let me take you back to when I was about 13/14 years old.

Leaving Monkton Park Primary school in Chippenham I took that big step into secondary school that all have done and will do. Off I went to Sheldon Comprehensive School. In my mind, I knew I was not the most academic person in the world and I also knew I could not find interest in sports. This for me played on my mind as I was trying to answer all those adults that ask you "what do you want to do or be when you leave school?". My answer was always "I don't know – I just don't know". I did not know, I had no idea, but then does anyone really know? Some of my friends would say – work in hospitals, be a policeman, be a teacher etc.… none of which I had any interest in.

Starting at Sheldon at that age you are grouped into a class level. I was not in the top or the bottom – just average. I used to ask myself, does that make me average then? As a kid, I did not want to be labelled average so that is where my determination started to aspire to be better.

I would think about things deeply and try to understand how I could be better. Initially, it was, work harder in school so over the years I go up in the levels of the class grades.

I set about this but each year I would remain in the average classes. This always just frustrated me, and I continued to ask – how in the hell do I do better if some things just do not sink in. I didn't really enjoy the academic lessons, but I did love the arts and drama side of school.

At this age, I was a confident little kid. Most things wouldn't phase me in the slightest which I put down to my parents as they both have the same mind set and hold the same confidence.

During the school holidays I would spend time going to work with my Dad, he had a tool hire shop opposite the hospital that mum worked at. I would go to the shop with him in the mornings and my mum would finish nights over the road and then start work again in the shop.

I thought she was amazing, as in my eyes, this lady did not need sleep (I laughed all the time thinking that she was wonder woman). I know my work ethic comes from both my parents.

During this time, I remember things at home changing slightly. Just the mood of things and sensed that things were getting hard for my parents.

I vaguely remember hearing conversations along the lines of…

"We are hitting hard times", "The country is a mess", "People owe us money and now they have gone bust and we won't get any of it".

I didn't really understand the severity of it then.

I remember my Dad saying he was closing the shop because he had so many people going bust on him that owed him money and he did not want the same to happen to him. He was proud and part of the local Lions Club. He wanted to hold his head up high knowing that he did the right thing, and he did.

He told me he was closing the shop and would make sure he makes everyone happy that he owes money to.

All this time I would say to myself that when I grow up, I hope I am not faced with these challenges and have to deal with this sort of thing.

Still at school, I was still in the average classes – still not moving up the levels but I knew I was still a good person deep down.

Dad's shop closed and I could sense the worry and frustration in both my parents, but one fundamental thing I will always remember is that they were together and happy, and they were in everything together, good, and bad.

We still had our caravan holidays – they still put me and my brother first. Teaching us morals and loyalty was such a great strength of theirs.

I never forget the day of going to the shop with Dad and helping to pack everything in boxes and vacating the premises and storing all the stock at home that he had remaining.

Mum was still working lots of nights as a sister at the hospital. She was a trooper for as long as I can remember.

Back at school – going into another year, remaining

in the same class level, I became so frustrated and quickly realised I was never going to be a lawyer or a doctor, so I needed to start thinking, what am I good at. I hated sports and only really continued to like the arts side of things. The only thing I did realise, I was good with others, I was confident and didn't really care what people thought. These thoughts remained at the forefront and I kept thinking, surely being a people's person I can do something good.

Dad got a great new job and my summers at the shop went, but I stayed going to work with him during the holidays. Travelling around the South West of England (this was his area he worked in) seeing so many different companies. He always seemed so happy at the start and end of the day.

We would go to Bournemouth and at lunchtimes go to a place called 'Viewpoint' in Poole where we would have a sausage sandwich from the burger van and then sit overlooking Poole harbour. Watching all the boats sailing in and out of the port. That place gave me such an amazing feeling which is where the start of the sea and coast became a love of mine. It felt so open and relaxed. I wanted more of that.

We would travel back home each day and I loved being out and about going to so many different towns and cities. I began to think, "maybe this is something I would really like to do".

Approaching my third year at school, it was options time! What subjects do I want to do? I had no idea so went with the subjects that I liked or had to do.

I had a strong affiliation to take Geography and the Arts. Having to take a science out of Physics, Biology or Chemistry!!! I went with Physics for the pure reason I thought it would be the easiest… how wrong was I.

During my fourth year, I hated Physics but remained with the love of drama and dance and the arts. Was this the route I should take?

As part of a school project, we had to create a small company in groups. Our group decided to sell cans of drink at break times. I was so happy that we would buy cans for a few pence and sell them for double. This was my first thoughts of "Ahhh this is how people make money". I loved being behind the stand selling to the other students and making the money.

At the end of the project, our group won and made the most profit of them all. This gave me a huge boost and made me realise that I was good at something.

That something was selling.

I started to investigate what qualifications were needed for selling. Delighted to find out that no real grades or qualifications were needed. This was a breath of fresh air to me... it took the pressure off me, so I could just enjoy the lessons and I developed the attitude of, whatever happens, I know I can do something. Learn products and sell them.

During that fourth year everything was still the same apart from my attitude. I had a clear view of things for the future:

1. Travel for work
2. Learn products and sell them!
3. Being confident should be a bonus!
4. Liking people should go in my favour!

These few things I believed I could take from school no matter what my grades would be. Alongside all my thoughts, every day I would be listening to all my friends talking about what they would do in 6th form and potentially university. I simply had no interest in this because in my mind I could not make money in the 6th form or at university. That route in my mind was for the aspiring doctors, dentists and lawyers. I wanted out asap, I wanted to earn money.

My GCSE's approached and I knew in my mind that I had no idea what the results would be. I sat the exams and, in every exam, I kind of smiled to myself thinking, this is no good, my grade will be rubbish but I don't need this for selling products. A lot of guessing went on in my exams and I would finish them quicker than anyone else in those examination rooms. I sat pretending that I was still answering the questions but all I was doing was thinking about what companies I could approach to learn about products. I would be thinking – what products do I want to sell and who can teach me.

If I recall, my final exam was English Language. I enjoyed this subject but still finished the exam early. It was during this exam that I realised I needed to go somewhere that I could learn about a variety of categories and where could I do that? A department store.

My Mum loved Jolly's in Bath, I did too. It was a real statement shop in the city loved by so many people. I had it in my head that once my results come through, I would call them to ask if they did any courses to learn all the categories.

Results Day: I went to the school with a few friends who were all so nervous. I remember my closest friend, Mike, saying to me, "are you nervous", I replied with as very direct "No way". I said I just wanted to get them, see what disasters I had achieved and want to go and earn money.

We all gathered in the school hall, in line to collect the little brown envelope. So many people opening theirs and smiling and cheering, mixed with people being disappointed. I opened mine and was pleasantly surprised. Given that I was expecting to get low grades, I achieved a mix of positive results. You know what – this was ok for me. The only one I was disappointed about was English with a D.

My instant reaction was – do not worry, go to college in the evening to re-sit this one for a year whilst I look for work.

I returned to do English at Chippenham Technical College (as it was named then). Every Thursday night and I was so delighted that a good friend at school was also doing this. She was great and we had such giggle every week doing our re-sit. I was not allowing this to stop me now.

So, I was straight on the phone. 1st call to Jolly's of Bath. (I had no understanding that it was owned by a company called House of Fraser. I did not understand at all why it said Jolly's over the door.)

There begins my next chapter in life: 'Life' being the key work.

2:
Life Begins...

Summer 1989. I made that call to the, what was then called, the personnel department at Jolly's in Bath asking about any jobs or training courses they did for retail. A lovely girl talked me through what sort of things they offer. I arranged to go and see her the following week where they explained about a great management course in retail they were doing. Time was of the essence as they started the course in two weeks.

I confirmed that day to start work with them in two weeks' time.

This was the start of my journey. I was so nervous on Day 1, walking into what seemed then, a huge department store, signing in at the staff entrance and being taken up to the personnel offices right at the top of this old building.

It was outlined to me what the next two years would entail and I had a rush of excitement. This was my first real job. An induction took place that week with me and the team of 6 of us who were on the course. An introduction to all the departments. The third day in we were introduced to the store manager, Mrs Shilma. A woman who entered the room and you knew she had arrived.

I just remember thinking – I want that level job.

For two years I spent working across all the different departments in store ranging from Menswear, Furniture, Lighting, Bedding, Cookware and Toiletries/Perfumery. Ending the course in Toiletries I suddenly had a huge passion for the products and the people in this department. I simply loved it and I realised at this point this type of product was what I loved. I would see the sales representatives of the brands we had in store coming in every 6-8 weeks to check on their brands. I knew then this was my way forward. But I was too young and needed more experience.

I used to speak to all the different sales reps and built a great relationship with them over time and they guided me as to where and what I needed to do. "Get experience" was all they said. "In as many places as you can".

Living at home with my parents was great but I just wanted my own space, my own place to do what I wanted and when I wanted. This was constant in my mind and therefore another reason I knew I had to make things work financially.

2 years on, I heard of a new store opening in Melksham called Leekes. The advert always made me smile – "Leekes, the out-of-town department store".

They had an open day one weekend to visit the site to explore work opportunities. I went on my own and met a great team of people who sat me down asking me what experience I had. I told them of my retail course I had completed at House of Fraser and they seemed pleased.

They were focussing on the soft furnishings and interior design department – which I only really had a small amount of experience in, but thought, what the hell. Let's do it. I applied for the job and received a letter in the post of asking me to join. I was overjoyed.

Two months on I started at Leekes in the Furnishings / Interiors department. Meeting all my new colleagues was daunting but I loved meeting the new people and very quickly built a great report with them all.

My boss at the time was a very strong lady called Sue. I loved Sue, but she was hard as nails and didn't mess about. I learnt then so much from her in how to be as a boss. Fair and firm.

After several months I got to know so many of the department managers and always thought, how do you get these manager jobs? I had an underlying determination that whatever I was doing, I wanted better. This feeling would not go away.

However, during my time here, I also had a bug inside of me that I wanted to go to Australia. I spent so long wondering how I could go there but to come back to a good job.

I said to myself – get the experience then go to Oz.

I did 2 years at Leekes and was ready to move on. It was now or never to travel.

My parents had very kindly built a fund for me which I was able to use for anything I wanted to – if it was sensible. It was about £800 which was a staggering amount to have then.

Deciding to leave Leekes and travel I booked an open return ticket to Australia for a year to work and travel.

The ticket cost around £500 leaving me some money to travel with but I knew I would need to work.

Arriving in Australia was amazing and after a few weeks, I wanted to get earning. The year ahead would become a huge learning curve in life. Learning about so many different people and different cultures, getting my hands dirty to earn money for the next leg of the travels.

Meeting family in Melbourne that I had not seen for years or even met before.

In Brisbane for my 21st birthday, I was then ready to head home and continue my wish and feeling to make a success.

I remember returning home and missing Australia so much - and the travelling. It was that, doing something different that I loved.

How could I take my little retail experience and merge it with excitement? No idea at this point to be honest. I just needed a job to earn money.

In the local paper, there was an advert to work at the local social security offices. I applied thinking I would not have a hope in hells chance. Went for the interview which I really enjoyed and hey presto got the job.

Starting in these offices was a completely different working practice to department stores. The people were much quieter, less elaborate, more reserved and the whole environment felt so uneventful to me.

I knew immediately it was not for me, but just thought I need the money so whilst here, keep my eyes out for something else.

Few months on I was so bored at work, nothing stimulated me at all, I needed out.

One afternoon I was on a tea break in the social security offices I was working in. In the staff room reading the paper, I spotted an advert for retail staff required onboard a UK ferry company.

That evening I wrote to the address in the paper from the advert and within days had a letter back to attend an interview in Southampton.

***

Just wanting to interrupt for a moment whilst writing this book: It is now the 29th December 2020 and we have all just experienced the strangest Christmas in recent times. Told not to mix, changes in the government's restrictions. Was 5 days of mixing, changed to just Christmas Day with three households and no overnights. What a world we are living in with the awful COVID-19.

The announcement of the delays in the schools returning: Only Primary, year 11 and 13 to return. All those that will be taking exams this coming year. I am listening to so many young people worried sick about what they will do and how they will do it. (It took me back to my thoughts in 1989 – albeit for different reasons. But the thoughts were the same).

I have been doing zoom calls with friends that have kids in school and hearing all the stories of their worries about exams, the results, and no job prospects. It has been great offering advice and suggestions to so many, look for the positive career paths – there are always some.

Now going back to that interview request…

***

I received the letter with the confirmed date and time to attend the interview for the ferry company. I was beyond excited and a little nervous. I wanted this job so badly.

That Saturday I went to "Burton" to buy a new suit and shirt for the interview. I had fire in my belly and wanted to make sure I made a great impression. First impressions count, I repeated to myself. Be Smart and show them what you are about. Be confident.

I had two weeks to prepare for the interview. I did as much research as I could at the library about ferries and what was onboard. I remembered as a kid going on ferries to France for holidays and remembered there were shops onboard. I thought it could be a good option for me if this is what they were looking for.

Interview day: I was so excited, I spent so long getting ready, ironing my shirt and tie to create a clean smart crisp look. (looking back now it was probably awful).

I drove to Southampton and arrived at the offices called "Quest". Entering the offices there were other people in the reception area, all of them looking like they were also there for an interview. I checked in with the lovely lady on reception as she requested that

I take a seat.

We were all called through to a room, which suddenly threw me, why are we all going through together. This is new to me. I was suddenly so nervous. We all sat down, and a chap walked in to welcome us and explained he would talk us through what is expected onboard and what opportunities they recruited for. He began sharing the different departments, cabins, restaurants, bars and retail. Bingo! The word retail struck a chord with me.

After about 45 minutes we were then called individually to have a one-to-one interview. I made it clear straight away I wanted to focus on the Retail side if that was possible. The lady explained they had several positions for the summer in the shops onboard. Perfect – I said in my head.

At the end of the interview, she stated that given I had experience in retail from House of Fraser and Leekes I would be going to the next stage.

She asked me to wait and meet with one of the team from P&O ferries.

This lovely lady called me through, and we just chatted like we had known each other for so long. She explained the long hours, hard graft expected and that it was very different to working in a store on land. This excited me more, something different.

I felt it went well and completed the interviews, then it was a waiting game. The following week I received the letter to be told I had been accepted and that I would need to go back to the Quest office to have a medical and to complete a fire fighting and sea survival course.

This was amazing for me. I completed the courses two weeks later and was then given my start date of my first ship. I thought all my dreams had come true.

I gave my notice to the social security office and focussed 100% on my new opportunity.

It was my first day of heading to the port to join the new ship. I had met a guy on the sea survival course, and he offered for me to stay with him the night before our first induction day.

We travelled from Fareham over to Portsmouth ferry terminal to meet our ship. P&O Pride of Portsmouth. We met a chap who took us down to the ship to get settled in for our three-day induction.

It was horrible being that new boy. Not having a clue what to expect but I still had the excitement, so I knew I was doing the right thing. The induction was a tour of the ship, through the whole front of house and behind the scenes. I was so happy and felt at home. Everyone was lovely and it felt like I had entered a new family of people in a micro world.

Three days onboard, in the conference room for the induction was amazing, I absorbed everything and could not wait to get my teeth into things. The final day I was given my ship and start date. It was the Pride of Portsmouth the following week.

Having collected all my new uniform – I was ready.

Joining the ship on the following Wednesday, I was ready. That was the start of something great. Joining the Retail onboard I began to have the time of my life. Meeting so many new people, my confidence just grew and grew. Over the coming years my determination for bettering myself stayed. I was assigned to go to other ships and after a couple of years began to step up to shop supervisor. I loved it, having more responsibility just drove me more.

I was then on the Pride of Bilbao and was asked to step up to Retail Manager for a couple of weeks which made my day. I was so proud of myself getting the new uniform which was so smart and with the gold stripes. I felt I had achieved something.

After a few amazing years on this ship, I was ready to further myself and really focus on a career.

My big learnings from my time at sea were, I knew I could sell, I loved managing people, I was beyond organised and I could drive a team to get results. Topped with loving the beauty category, this gave me the direction and foundation I needed for the next step.

I began to apply for sales representative posts and was advised to get the Grocer magazine every Saturday. I applied for so many even though the adverts clearly stated sales rep experience was required. Every beauty product application, I just didn't get interviews for. I began to diverse my applications and came across an advert for Hallmark Gifts. I knew the company name from the cards and was not aware this was a separate business. I applied and got the interview which was at the head office in Tewkesbury.

Within days I was offered the job which I was ecstatic about as this would be my big step on the sales career ladder. I was at this point following my father as it was a sales representative post covering the south west of England. By now I had moved to Bournemouth, renting a flat but I was desperate to buy my own. This job would be the catalyst in me doing this.

My company car arrived; I could not believe it. I was given a car for my job. Back then this was a huge thing as I had never owned a brand-new car. My white Mondeo sat on the drive and I was so proud.

I went on so many sales courses with Hallmark to gain as much experience as possible. I loved travelling around the south west of the country, staying in hotels working away. Meeting all my customers and building such amazing relationships with them.

After a year in the job, I applied for my first ever mortgage which was accepted. It felt such an achievement. I purchased a ground floor, one-bedroom flat between Southbourne and Boscombe just on the outskirts of Bournemouth. I loved it and this was my first home.

Few months down the line I was at one of my customers in Plymouth – Derry's Department store (no longer there) where I met one of the Hallmark Gifts National Account Managers. She was a nightmare and even the store staff told me they could not stand her visiting. She was simply rude and was on a power trip. I knew I could do that job ten times better than her but just needed to be given the chance. I quizzed her as to how she got the national job and just zapped all information I could from her.

I knew I needed to get some different experience in different companies to get to the national level.

With my training, and now good experience, I applied to companies' ad-hock, asking them to consider me for any post should they come available. I didn't realise at the time, but this initiative was so important for me going forward. I literally took addresses off the packaging of products I liked and sent my CV to their head offices.

One of these products was a spa brand I spotted in a pharmacy in Cornwall. Aquae Sulis.

I was immediately attracted to the packaging and the smell of the products. I subsequently sent a letter and CV to them and got a reply a few weeks later asking me to go to Reading for an interview for an area sales manager post.

***

Little note here: had I not sent this letter and CV off my own back I would never have been asked to go and meet them.

***

I met the team who were amazing and had the interview. We clicked and I loved the passion for the brand and the products. I felt something about the beauty industry that had not left me since the time at House of Fraser.

This was the real start of my beauty career. I adored the brand and selling it to salons, spas and pharmacies across the South of England. I was so determined to be successful and get the brand into as many places as possible.

During my time here, and in all the sales meetings we would have, I felt I had such good ideas to implement but I would go home asking myself, why won't people listen?

It was the company way or no way. This to me was wrong, why not bring everyone's ideas together to make things better. Frustration began to set in and yet my determination stayed with me. 2 years on I knew my ideas would never be taken on board so it was my time to move on. I took this as an opportunity to step up and go to the next best level.

I noticed an advert for regional sales managers for a new innovative salon treatment that was launching and had been created by a team of people from the medical world. A spectrum light that was used to smooth wrinkles around the eye area. Sounds good hey!

I won't dwell on this – but I got the job covering the south of England, selling this new treatment machine into salons. Successfully, I sold it to most of the salons I had a relationship with from my previous job.

6 months in I was promoted to Southern Regional Sales Manager, managing the team of area sales managers, 6 in total. This was amazing from a personal perspective as this was the next career experience steppingstone for me.

A year on, I and one colleague realised something was wrong! Hundreds of complaints that the treatment did not work and everyone requesting refunds. This was a difficult time, but I managed it well however under no illusion that if this carried on there would not be a business. I managed to get hold of the trials document and in amazement, discovered that it was trialled on only 7 people, all women, non-smokers and never really went in the sun. Alarm bells kicked in……

I left this role to look for my next venture.

3:

Entering National But Followed By Mistakes

As I had previously done, I sent letters and my CV to lots of companies and promptly got a reply from a local beauty business – Bomb Cosmetics.

I now had national and regional management experience and delighted to join these guys as UK National Account Manager. For that time, it was a wow salary and enabled me to move home to a larger flat within a short walk to the Beach.

For nearly 4 years I build a great business across the national retailers in the UK and was now selling to the likes of Debenhams, House of Fraser, Superdrug and Sainsburys. Dealing with the big boys was very different but I loved it. It gave me such satisfaction seeing the brand appear on the shelves of these big retailers, knowing it was me that had done this.

Once again after time, frustration began to grow in

seeing a company not wanting to change or meet the requirements of what these retailers needed. I also had a vision that I wanted to do something different and to combine my experience and wishes.

Sunday afternoons I would meet friends for drinks in the garden at The Dormy Hotel in Ferndown and I remember saying to them, "One day I want to live in an area just like this, surrounded in huge trees and a sought after area". This is a very pivotal point for later in my career!

By this point, my parents had recently moved to Spain where I was spending a lot of time and long weekends.

I decided I wanted to run and own a bar in the sun!

I sold my flat, gave my notice and started planning to move to Spain. Looking at so many different places to lease to open a bar by the water.

I was delighted to have made a profit on my flat of nearly £40K which I could use for the bar in Spain. This is really where my internal business learnings began.

Everything was packed ready to be collected to go to

Spain. Flights all booked and ready to go.

Arriving in Spain was a great feeling, but I knew this is where the hard work begins. On finding an old run-down bar I quickly signed a contract to rent the property and went about renovating it and turning it into a trendy local wine bar. I employed a couple of people and got the stock in.

The bar opened and was exactly how I imagined it to look. That was just the beginning. Bar Oceana was born. Situated on the Mar Menor near La Manga. Perfect. So, I thought.

I quickly realised, the two staff members were not who I thought they were, not only were they lazy they were taking money from the till (albeit I could not prove it).

My savings were becoming low from all the outlay I had done, but we started to earn which was great.

Stupidly I did not get the contract looked at by an English lawyer, until now. I was becoming close to the end of year one of the contract and asked a UK lawyer to look at it for me. I was shocked at what I had signed.

I take full responsibility: but after year 1 the landlord had the rights to take back the bar and run it himself with giving me three months' notice to leave but I had no rights over any of the fixtures, fitting, or stock. I had truly been drawn into a huge issue. I had 6 weeks to decide what I was to do.

My feelings were: It's my mistake, I can make this good. I am not enjoying it so get out whilst I can. Put it down to one of life's horrid experiences.

Within 72 hours I decided to close the bar. Give the landlord the required 4 weeks' notice and plan a return to the UK. I found a company to buy all the equipment I had in the bar and the stock. They bought the lot for 15K.

They arrived and cleared the bar and gave me the cash.

On one hand, I was totally gutted that the landlord had driven me to this, but on the other hand, I thought – at least this is my money, and I do not owe a bank anything.

I knew that I had a few good contacts back in the UK so took the decision to return and focus on what I loved – the beauty industry.

U Can Do It

***

It is now Monday 4th January 2020! Where the country would normally return to work and the new year really begins in our economy. Yet many schools are closed, and delays of different years not returning to their education and a return to home schooling. Another huge blow for all our countries students. Leaving them again in the unknown. We have also just been informed that Scotland will return to a full national lockdown as from tomorrow (5th January) for the full month with the view that continuing the lockdown is an option into February.

This virus is out of control and we believe the country has the view that our government has lost control too. I am hearing more stories of students, weather in first, secondary or university, that they are worried about their futures and the exam period of 2021.

All more reason for me to give confidence in these people to read that, no matter what – U Can Do It…!

***

On returning to the UK in 2005, I had approximately 8K in the bank and no job. Time to make things happen and fast.

My closest friend and his wife kindly offered for me to stay with them until I found myself a decent job. This is when and where close friends come in to their own and I knew I was incredibly lucky to have Mike and Wendy at this time in my life.

I set out contacting all the recruitment agents I knew and fired out my CV to hundreds of companies. Location was not an issue and I was prepared to move and live anywhere in the UK for the right role.

Very quickly I was offered two NAM (National Account Manager) roles, (I should reiterate though, I must have sent out over 200 letters and CV), one with a soap manufacturing business based just outside of Leicester and another role with Grosvenor, the gift toiletries division of Hasbro – the games and toy giants. I took the Grosvenor job as I thought this would suit me better.

I started the job and very quickly realised I had made a mistake. The office was full of very nice people, but everyone wanted the loudest voice to be heard. There was no teamwork, it was all about having a 'me' view. I didn't like that environment and only I could change that. So, I continued to explore the options coming through to me from all the application I had previously sent out.

One evening after being so deflated with the management at work, I received a call from a recruitment agent asking me if I was keen to meet a company in West London for a NAM role, a beauty accessories business. Explaining that I had just started a new job, they swiftly arranged an interview for me the following week.

I remember turning up to a warehouse on an industrial estate (far from the glam I had hoped for in the industry) for the interview with Original Additions.

Entering reception, I was greeted so kindly from the receptionist and offered a coffee or tea. She was lovely and I remember thinking, if the people here are all like her then I love it already.

The Sales Director came to meet me, and we went through to the meeting room where he made me feel so welcome and comfortable. We got on like a house of fire and spoke for 2 hours in-depth about me and my background and about Original Additions. I fully understood what they were looking for and their goals. I knew immediately I wanted the job and, in my head, driving away that day from their car park, I knew I had to nail the second interview that Mark had already said I had got.

The recruitment agency called me immediately asking me to go back for the second interview on the Friday of this week. They requested I prepare a presentation to give to Mark and this could be on anything I wished.

As soon as got home, laptop open, I started on my presentation. For me, I needed to get across to Mark why the company needed me and nobody else. That formed my subject to present. To present Mark Wood, calling it a presentation of Innovation and Inspiration.

I took my time in researching Original Additions and it's brands. Seeing where the brands were and where they could be. More importantly, where I believed I could take them. I also focussed on what Mark said in the first interview. They were a business that ran like a family, the teams all got on so well and worked very much in collaboration as one business. One of my own personal preferences in a company and how I love to work.

Presentation done; I was prepped. The second meeting with Mark was like we had known each other for months as I set out presenting my slides.

At the end, Mark simply said: Brilliant Mark, I am so

impressed. He followed up with, "what is your availability"?

The recruitment agent called which was followed by an email job offer. I was delighted to know I could give my notice to a company I just did not like. This all happened very quickly and before I knew it, I was on my first day at Original Additions.

What a fantastic bunch of people, I knew I had made the right choice. I said to myself, I could see myself here for a few years. This was May 2005.

By 2008 I was loving the teams but felt the company was a little disjointed. Totally unaware of what it was, but I just had a negative feeling. In the summer of 2007, I was offered a job with Coty, a company I knew of very well, a big name in the industry. However, I also knew I did not really want to leave my team. Coty gave me a couple of weeks to decide and at this point, I came down with a heavy fever and was signed off work for three weeks.

During my last week of being off sick, I decided to accept the Coty job and on my return from sick leave, I would proceed reluctantly in giving my notice.

All typed up and ready to give it to Mark, I arrived at

the office to be told Mark was working from home as he was not too well.

I sat at my desk, mind running at a thousand miles an hour, wondering if to give the letter to Simon (Managing Director). I really didn't want to as Simon and I got on so well.

What to do?...

4:
It All Changed From Here...

Holding my resignation letter in my hand, sat at my desk, Simon wandered over to me and asked if he could see me privately in his office for a chat. I popped the letter inside my jacket pocket and went to his office.

A cup of tea waiting, and a smile greeted me. He was and still is a real gent.

He explained to me that there were changes happening in the business at board level and that my boss (Sales Director) had decided to exit the business as the company was entering a re-finance process. Followed up with asking me if would be interested in taking over the Sales Director post and join the board of directors. To also buy into the business so I had the benefits of long-term success through any future processes the company engaged with.

***

Now coming back to me writing this: Today is the 5th of January and last night Boris Johnson announced that the UK will enter a new national lockdown and all schools will close as from the 7th January until mid-February. All non-essential businesses to also close as we return to what we had in March last year. A devastating blow as they also announce that students due to take their GCSE's this year will all now not take place. Another year of worry and uncertainty for our school leavers in 2021. I must get this finished to share the positivity of what is out there for anyone.

***

So, back to my pivotal moment in my career of being offered the Sales Director and investor post. I was overjoyed and obviously accepted immediately. Knowing I could make decisions, run a team, and make a difference took my drive to another level.

Early during 2008 I signed the papers and joined the board. This was it for me and my motivation was at a level I did not think could exist. Pulling my team together giving them the confidence in what we were about to embark on and changes that I would make to allow us all to thrive.

This was my first experience of being in a board meeting. I remember the first meeting being incredibly nervous, something I never really was as I had always created my own comfort zone. I sat there as all the other directors arrived along with our investors. Honestly, I had no idea what to expect or how to be. I said to myself… Now Mark, be yourself, be confident and just remember I know more about the sales side of this business than them.

We kicked off with the Chairman opening the meeting and passing to the MD for a business overview. Then one by one went around the board table with each director giving a full update of their division. Then my tern. I stumbled a little but then very quickly began talking about where the business was to date but more importantly where I wanted to take it. Sharing my plans. This was the first time I ever remember truly being listened to. The full board supported everything I said and everything I wanted to do. I knew at that point I had hit my golden ticket – I was being fully trusted to move this business forward, both on the sales side but also the team. Building a strong division with the right people in the right jobs driving the business forward.

The following few years were amazing and I was introduced to the format of 'collaborations' in business. We were the first in our category to do a celebrity collaboration. We embarked on a business journey with the biggest Girl Band of that time – Girls Aloud. Meeting with the girls to create a unique false lash range to bring to the market for the consumer. The girls were great and designed their own products and packaging design for the collection which we delivered into the market. This was the start of a great business relationship with some of the girls, one more than the others!

U Can Do It

Launch of our Girls Aloud collaboration

Nadine and I clicked, we just got each other even though we had minimal communication at the start of the project.

This friendship began to grow and myself and my partner began having dinner and evenings with Nadine and our friendship blossomed. As it still stands today – one amazing, talented friend who believes in people and does not put fame at the forefront.

The collaborations continued over the years and we teamed up with Katy Perry, Paris Hilton, Ben Cohen, Little Mix, Paloma Faith and Emma Willis. What a great few year it became.

U Can Do It

Premier of the Katy Perry movie that we sponsored

Launch of our Little Mix collaboration

As social media influencers became so much more prevalent in the beauty world, we expanded our partnerships and signed with the likes of Fleur De Force, Jordyn Woods and several bloggers in the USA.

At this point, I stopped and thought back to my leaving school days. Saying to myself – wow, would I ever have thought I would be at this position in a large business dealing with the world of celebrity. I had to pinch myself and tell myself it was down to my determination and hard work I had put in over the years. I was loving life.

Good friend Ben Cohen after our collaboration

U Can Do It

Good friend Nadine Coyle at my wedding!

In 2015, in one of our monthly board meetings, we agreed that we would begin a process and compile our IM (Information Memorandum) to commence a sale of the business. We all spent months putting this together and the business went to market later in 2015. Very quickly we had some great responses, one, a large beauty company based in Stamford USA. PDC Brands.

The team from PDC arrived in early 2016 to meet us to begin discussions for them to acquire Original Additions. Things moved fast – very fast. After that one-week visit, offers began to flow across the pond for our company. We all agreed on a figure and the company merger completed in just a few months and the deal was done in April 2016.

We celebrated like crazy, my moment of thinking back to when I invested and had the opportunity to take over the sales director post came flooding back and to then see the rewards of the payment, I received on the sale completion. I never thought my bank account would look like it did, leaving school with very average results and not knowing what I would be doing with my life.

It had always been my dream to own a large boat, this was our first purchase. I could not believe myself and my partner were viewing 40-50ft boats, I was beside myself with happiness.

We purchased a beautiful Sealine F42 for a large sum of money! that was only 4 years old, she became my baby and gave me such joy as a boat owner.

*My pride and joy. The first motorboat we purchased.
MY Ceapairean II*

U Can Do It

MY Ceapairean II

Simon (MD) and I continued to stay with the newly merged business whilst three other directors left to explore new opportunities.

From a personal level, you may remember earlier I mentioned about living in a nice sought-after area! Early in 2017, I knew I had been successful, and my reward was to also find that dream home I had always wished for.

One Sunday afternoon, my partner and I drove past the old site of The Dormy Hotel where I used to drink beer in the garden. I was overjoyed that there was a new show home with a stunning collection of houses on. We viewed the show home and by April 2017 we were moving in. I could not believe it, thinking back to those days when it was the hotel dreaming of living in a place like this. It happened.

Simon and I became even closer and we knew things would be different and that we would potentially have to change the way we do things to meet the USA ways of working. 6 months in, we both knew it was not the same and the culture differences were like chalk and cheese between ourselves and the USA office. We knew the control had left us and shifted to our sister office in the US, moving forward any decision making would sit with them. Both Simon and I faced these challenges and understood that there needed to be some change.

During 2017: The full PDC business went up for sale. The company was owned by a private equity house, and they decided to sell PDC to another private equity group. The great thing was, we had another pay-out to look forward to as shareholders in the business.

I received a call one evening as we were approaching the completion of the deal from our existing PE house. I liked these guys, very down to earth and understood the business. Then came the request. They asked me to remain with the group and take over as Managing Director as Simon had decided to exit. One side of me was gutted as Simon was one of my anchors, and the other side of me was beyond excited at this top-level role I knew I could love and get my teeth in to. Once again taking my approach and making changes where needed to really get the success.

I slept on it and accepted the offer of MD the following day.

Two months later, the deal completed, I received a further payout which really gave me another huge boost. I took on the MD role and very quickly made changes, bought the two offices closer together, as we expanded the business. Fast forward a couple of years and I had successfully built the business, brands and the teams to the level I desired. For me at this point I had really become a filter, with everything coming to me from the USA, I chose what I shared with my full team to ensure their motivation remained. This was really going against my ethos and values as I have always been about 'honesty is the best policy'. However, I knew the team would become depressed, demotivated, and very despondent if they knew it all. This was the time for me to take some time out and enjoy business again.

I called the CEO and asked if we could look at exit options. It was my time to move on and enjoy life and do something new.

Thankfully, down to my own hard work, determination, and motivation, I was in a wonderful position to do this, due to the drive I had. Which I still have to this day.

I exited the business in 2019, spending the summer of that year on my boat in the South of France, planning out what I wanted to do, for me.

One thing to always remember is that you never stop

learning, whether that be in business or about people. Leadership was one thing I loved over the years, and am good at it, driving a team of people. Really being generous and giving credit where credit is due. Giving people chances and in many cases 2nd or 3rd chances. I did learn a big thing in leadership, do not give too much, as it, or you are not so appreciated later down the line.

Don't get me wrong, looking back over 30 years I have made my fair share of mistakes and wrong decisions however I have learnt from this and to ensure I wouldn't repeat these.

Even afterwards, was I level-headed? Yes. Was I honest with myself and others? Yes. Did I correct myself? Yes. Did I believe in myself? Yes.

Getting the opportunity to write this book was driven by the ambition and determination that I have written about. Even today, after my great successes, I know I have not reached my pinnacle. Still having that fire in my belly, I had all those years ago to continue creating and taking brands and companies beyond their expectations.

It's like having a travel bug! Once it's in you, it never leaves you.

That fire in my belly has enabled me to continue working with several beauty brands, giving my knowledge and background experience to businesses that are new and entering the retail world today. It gives me such pleasure and satisfaction that I am making a difference.

Today, launching a wonderful Spanish premium skin care brand called, 'Skin Generics' globally. Helping a great men's skin protection brand, 'Lifejacket', enter the retail market in the UK along with investing and supporting my other half with his on-line marine business, 'Boat-Central.com'. To become the largest UK boat owner's website. A wonderful mix with wonderful people giving me a career cocktail I could only have dreamt of years ago, Boats and the Beauty Industry!

All this is down to the fact I said to myself in 1989: "U Can Do It Mark and only one person can make it happen…U".

I truly hope this short book of inspiration will help students if they have the same mind as I did at leaving school. In just the past few weeks I have spoken to parents giving advice on companies their kids should approach. Even in these bad times, there are lots of companies and industries doing well and I have listed just a few ideas that I hope could help.

The Grocery sector is strong, we have some of the biggest grocers in the world and careers with them are prosperous. Online retail is beyond positive, we have many great on-line retailers in the UK who are growing at accelerated rates, these are great businesses to join and be part of. If I.T/comms is your thing, our recent times have made on-line comms grow at a crazy rate with the owners of video conferencing being a solid career path for many.

From a category perspective, there are some great product areas that are performing well and always a good approach. Health and Beauty, Food and Drink, Technology, Household goods, DIY and Garden equipment are all areas that have done incredibly well through these tougher times.

Don't rely on the business social network sites that are advertising hundreds of jobs, many of which are through recruitment agents who never get back to you. They are not all reliable. Get your CV out to as many companies directly, and you will receive the rewards.

Be positive, persistent, and motivated. Remembering one thing, U Can Do It…!

Available worldwide from
Amazon and all good bookstores

---

www.mtp.agency

www.facebook.com/mtp.agency

@mtp_agency

Michael Terence
Publishing

www.ingramcontent.com/pod-product-compliance
Lightning Source LLC
LaVergne TN
LVHW011740060526
838200LV00051B/3268